Greatest Heroes and Legends OF THE BIBLE

Joseph and the Coat of Many Colors

retold by Ellen Titlebaum
illustrated by Kallen Godsey

inchworm PRESS
™

Long ago, in the land of Canaan, an old shepherd named Jacob lived with his many sons. The newest addition to the family was Benjamin. "Benjamin looks just like Joseph did when he was a baby," said Jacob to his wife, Rachel. "I wonder what's taking the older boys so long to gather the wheat. Joseph?" called Jacob.

"Yes, father . . . ."

"Make sure your brothers are seeing to their work."

"Yes father, right away," said Joseph.

"If only my older sons were more like him," said Jacob, watching Joseph make his way across the dry fields.

When Joseph reached the fields, he found his older brothers playfully throwing sheaves of wheat at each other. "What's going on here!" cried Joseph just as Reuben walloped Simeon. The remaining brothers jumped in for a boisterous pillow fight using bundles of wheat.

"Look at that! It's father's little spy!" taunted Simeon.

"You guys were supposed to have this wheat loaded hours ago. Let me help you," said Joseph.

Reuben picked up a sheaf of wheat and threw it. It hit Joseph in the chest, knocking him down. All of his brothers laughed.

"You wouldn't laugh so hard if you knew what I dreamt last night!" said Joseph. "We were all in the fields making sheaves of wheat, when suddenly one of my sheaves leapt out of my hands. Then, your bundles formed a circle around mine, and bowed down to my bundle."

"Joseph expects us to bow down to him!" cried Reuben. "Let's get him!" The brothers formed a circle around Joseph, and began to push and taunt him. Scared, Joseph broke free and ran off.

The next morning, Jacob presented Joseph with a coat of many colors. Unlike the robes Joseph's brothers wore, this had long sleeves, the sign of princely fashion. It sparkled.

"When my brothers see me wearing such a fine coat—" said Joseph.

"They will understand, my son," said Jacob, helping Joseph into the rich fabric. "Your brothers are tending the flock. Go keep an eye on them."

Joseph's brothers were sitting in the field, watching Joseph make his way over a hill to reach them. "Look at that coat!" cried Asher. "We wear rags, and he dresses like a prince!"

"This is the last straw. I've had enough of father's favorite son, Joseph," said Simeon.

When Joseph reached his brothers, they threw him to the ground and ripped off his coat of many colors. Ignoring Joseph's pleas, his brothers

dropped him into a dark pit. "That's for turning father against us!" shouted Reuben into the black hole.

"I bet the Ishmaelite traders will pay good money for him," said Judah. The brothers sold Joseph for twenty pieces of silver, and he was taken to Egypt as a slave.

Then they dipped his coat in goat's blood, and took it home to Jacob. "My son! My son!" wailed Jacob. "A wild animal must have eaten him!" It seemed that Jacob's grief would never end.

Joseph, now a slave, was bought by Potiphar, the Pharaoh's Captain of the Guards. "I am pleased with your work, Joseph," said Potiphar. "You're smarter than my other slaves. I'm putting you in charge of my household."

"I'll do my best to serve you," said Joseph respectfully.

Years passed happily in Potiphar's household, and Joseph grew into an attractive young man. One day, while Joseph was working in the garden, Potiphar's wife strolled up to him.

"I've had my eye on you for some time," she whispered.

"I, uh, think I should get back to work," Joseph stammered.

"Take me in your arms and kiss me! I order you to!" she cried.

"I can't," said Joseph.

"Then I'll tell Potiphar you did anyway! You'll be thrown in jail!" she shrieked.

As she threatened, Potiphar's wife made sure that Joseph was thrown in prison. One day, Joseph stopped by the Royal Cupbearer's cell to listen to him describe a dream he had.

"I was in the Pharaoh's field, tending to a vine with three branches, when the buds suddenly blossomed and ripened into grapes! So, I squeezed the grapes into his cup, and gave it to the Pharaoh to drink. What do you think it means?" asked the Cupbearer.

"The three branches of the vine represent three days," said Joseph. "In three days you will be pardoned, and returned to your position as Cupbearer to the Pharaoh."

"In my dream," said the Baker, "I had three baskets filled with breads for the Pharaoh. Birds flew out of the sky and ate all of the breads."

"In three days you will be hanged, by orders of the Pharaoh," said Joseph quietly.

And so it happened. Three days later, the Cupbearer was called back to court, and the Baker was hanged.

Two years later, the Pharaoh dreamed that he was standing on the banks of the Nile when seven healthy cows came out of the water followed by seven skinny cows. Then, the skinny cows ate the healthy cows!

Later, he had another dream. Seven ears of corn, large and golden, grew out of the ground. But then, seven sickly ears of corn grew up and ate the healthy corn.

The Pharaoh was troubled by his dreams. He called all his wise men together to interpret them, but no one could help him. Then the Cupbearer remembered Joseph.

Joseph was taken from prison and placed before the Pharaoh at his great court.

"God is telling you what he intends to do," explained Joseph. "The seven healthy cows and ears of corn mean seven years of abundance. The seven sick cows and ears of corn mean seven years of famine. My Lord, you need to collect food now while it's plentiful to prepare for the famine."

"Joseph, you will be in charge of collecting the food. You are now the high governor of Egypt," said the Pharaoh.

Joseph filled up Egypt's barns with food. And then, famine struck! But, thanks to Joseph, Egypt was prepared.

Soon, the famine spread into Canaan, where Jacob and his sons lived. Jacob sent his oldest sons to Egypt to buy food, but insisted that his youngest son, Benjamin, stay with him.

One day, Joseph was standing outside of one of his storehouses, when he spotted his brothers, waiting to buy grain. Joseph pretended that he did not recognize them. He cried out, "These men are spies!"

His brothers were surrounded by guards! "We're not spies!" said Reuben.

"Do you have any other brothers?" asked Joseph, softly.

"Our youngest brother, Benjamin, stayed at home," said Reuben.

"You will bring this youngest brother to me," said Joseph.

"But my Lord, our father will never let him go!" cried Simeon.

"Guards, escort these men to jail!" commanded Joseph.

The brothers were thrown into the dungeon. Joseph stood outside their cell, listening in. "We're being punished for what we did to Joseph! We broke father's heart and made God angry with us!" sobbed Reuben.

Joseph, wiping a tear from his eye, stepped toward the cell. "If you bring me your youngest brother, I will let you go free. Simeon, you will stay behind."

As the brothers prepared for their journey, Joseph ordered his guards to fill their sacks with food and to return their silver.

When the brothers reached Canaan, Jacob opened the sacks of grain and found pouches of silver. "What is the silver doing here? Have we been tricked?" said Jacob. He knew that he had to let Benjamin go to Egypt to save Simeon and to get more food.

"Pack our best spices and bring them to the Ruler of Egypt as a gift. Here is double the silver. Don't let anything happen to Benjamin . . . or I will die in great sorrow," Jacob told his sons.

When the brothers returned to Egypt with Benjamin, Joseph prepared a great feast.

"Sir, when we returned home, we found that someone had secretly returned our silver. You may think we stole it, but I swear to you, we didn't! Please take it back!" pleaded Reuben.

"Do not worry. Is this your youngest brother?" asked Joseph.

"Yes, it is," said Reuben.

While the feast was served, Joseph turned to his guard and said, "Take my silver cup and put it in the younger brother's sack."

The next morning the brothers were stopped by the Governor's chariot. "Someone stole the master's silver cup!" cried the steward. "We must check your sacks of food!"

The steward found the silver cup in Benjamin's sack. "We'll let the Governor decide what to do about this!" he admonished them.

Joseph's brothers were kneeling before him at the palace. "Benjamin is the thief—he will stay behind as my slave!" ordered Joseph.

"The young boy means all the world to our father . . . our other brother was . . . killed. . . Our father never recovered. If he lost Benjamin, it would kill him!" sobbed Reuben.

"I can take this no longer! Come closer and look at me, my brothers! I am Joseph! The brother you sold to slavery! Because I could decipher the Pharaoh's dreams, he appointed me high Governor. I predicted the famine and made sure that Egypt was prepared. You see, it was God's plan all along. Go tell father the news and bring him and the family here, to live with me," said Joseph.

Then Joseph threw his arms around his brothers, and all was forgiven.